Relatable You

Real, Relatable Rhymes

Jaycee Michaels

ISBN: 978-1-7395739-0-4

DEDICATION

In memory of my little brother.
I dedicate my book to you.
Thank you for our bond.
I will love you forever.
Terry Michael.

TABLE OF CONTENTS

ACKNOWLEDGEMENTS

I would like to express my deepest appreciation to my editor, Danielle Kenyon.
The completion of this book would not have been possible without her hard work and dedication.

To Louise Woodward, who informed me that I must write a book. I wasn't sure if it was optional, so I did as I was told!

Paula Wilson, Pam Woodward, Beccy Woodward, Kirsty Williams, Barbara McIntyre, and the one and only…. Joanne Kenny.

My gorgeous Mum & Stepdad,
Pat & Billy.

Thank you all so very much for your love and support.
It means the world.

My special thanks go to my beloved companion, Smokey.
(Yes Beccy, it goes to the cat!)
He has forfeited a lot of what he loves the most (after food), my attention. He has sat by my side for many hours while I stared at the computer instead of staring at him (like I usually do), and he has patiently (or not) listened to the same poems repeatedly.

CHAPTER ONE

GOODBYES

Chronicle of Grief

Bereavement, the grief when we lose someone dear,
an assortment of feelings mixed up and unclear.

When shock and numbness see the end of their day,
when reality sets in and won't go away.

These feelings then hit like a cruel ton of bricks,
they shake through your bones and they knock you for six.

Denial, for a while, will be your best friend,
but your time to pretend will come to an end.

When it's time to admit, it's happened, it's true,
don't know how to feel, what to think, what to do.

In any old order they come and they go,
each stage of this grief, a hard heavy blow.

At some point you'll bargain and drive yourself nuts,
with the shouldas, the couldas, the ifs and the buts.

When anger sets in and the world is to blame,
when your world falls apart at the sound of their name.

Guilt and regret, they come hand in hand,
and all of a sudden, it's you, you can't stand.

Your mind is invaded, self-hate and despair,
you should have stepped in, you should have been there.

Questions unanswered, will remain so,
mind is amok, as you just need to know.

Was he in pain? Was it quick? Was it slow?
Was he scared? Was he cold? Did he feel every blow?

Was he gasping for air? Was he fighting or crying?
Did he know he was loved? Did he know he was dying?

The sadness, it hurts and cuts deep to your core,
anguish so painful, no means to ignore.

When your eyes are heavy, when your head is sore,
when you've cried to the point where you can cry no
more.

Time is no healer and time is no friend,
the wounds they may heal but the scars they don't mend.

Depression, reflection, anxiety in tow,
mourning and misery, sorrow and woe.

Moving on, climbing out of your miserable hole,
acceptance and hope and rebuilding your soul.

A burdensome journey to heal your poor heart,
but crucial to try so the process can start.

Gain new ways to cope, to get through each day,
find new ways to think, to keep darkness at bay.

Learn to get by, to smile and to grow.
It's the story of grief, if you've lost then you know.

What's It Like in Heaven

What's it like in heaven? Are you waiting there for me?
Is it filled with ones we've lost? Is it as peaceful as can be?

Have your ailments been restored? Are you right back in your prime?
Is everything there beautiful? Are the views up there sublime?

Are you surrounded by great love? The kind of which, you're sure?
The kind that lasts forever? The kind that's true and pure?

Are the streets there lined with flowers? Is nature wild and free?
Is everyone there happy? Does everyone agree?

Is the sky there filled with rainbows? Is the water crystal clear?
Is your mind filled with contentment? Do you smile from ear to ear?

Does the sunlight shine more brightly there? Do the stars bewitch your soul?
Does your spirit feel enchanted? Does your heart feel full and whole?

Can you watch over your loved ones as and when you crave?
Do you find it hard to watch us when we're tearful at your grave?

Do you ever miss our company? Do you ever wish you'd stayed?
To continue on your journey, on the path from which you strayed.

I hope you don't feel guilty if you're happier up there,
I imagine such a wonder, one that someday we will share.

Till then, enjoy your time there and embrace the promised land,
for one day we will meet again and walk there hand in hand.

Broken Up and Bereft

"It's over, I'm done." Your last words to me,
in shock, I enquire, "how can this be?"

You cannot go on, you're walking away,
I'm frantic and panicked. I beg you to stay.

Failing to fathom why you'd leave me behind,
you fell out of love? Someone else on your mind?

How could you give up on all of our dreams?
Our plans for the future meant nothing, it seems.

I know this can work, I'll do better, do more,
like I would have, I could have, I should have before.

You'll rethink and regress, and I'll be waiting here,
no way are we done, you'll be back, I'll not fear.

But time's moving on, and I've not heard a word,
the silence is loud, and hope becomes blurred.

Denial has diminished, the truth it kicks in,
I feel sick, I feel sad, and my head's in a spin.

I hate you, I'm angry, for wasting my prime,
negative thoughts fill my mind and my time.

Rejection is rampant, my ego is bruised,
you cannot have loved me, I'm lost and confused.

Are you online? I can't help but explore,
our pictures, our memories, cut deep to the core.

No longer our song, no longer our place,
our bond traded in for distance and space.

Are you okay? I worry and wonder,
on top of the world or regretting your blunder?

Turning the page, a new chapter without you,
it doesn't feel right after all that we've been through.

But time to accept, move forward and mend,
forget about closure, it's over, the end.

Look to the future, ahead and not back,
the start has arrived, feeling good, back on track.

The light is restored, no longer depressed,
my heart is now healing. I wish you the best.

A Fading Farewell – (Dementia/Alzheimer's)

Unnoticed it crept in, so subtle and so sly,
the onset of the longest, and more than one goodbye.

Nothing too dramatic, minor details slipped your mind,
some things you'd never say and some things you could not find.

Then a little more confused, acting different than before,
walking after midnight, destination not quite sure.

What happened yesterday, you no longer could recall,
what tomorrow may bring in, was your affliction's call.

Then came the dreaded day, this illness raised the bar,
a vacant stare and painful words, "I don't know who you are."

Forgetting more than memories, the basics you once knew,
fading right before us was the light that made you, you.

Like dismantling a jigsaw, removing part by part,
till there was nothing left to take, but the beating of your heart.

CHAPTER TWO

PETS

I Pledge to Thee

I pledge to thee, I promise, to be a faithful friend.
Loyal I'll be, and judgement free, on me you can depend.

Reliable and ready, on hand to make you smile,
I'll walk beside you always, for a minute or a mile.

I'll miss you when you leave, every second you're away,
and I'll welcome you each time as though you've been gone for a day.

I'll add purpose to your life and bring you comfort when you're low,
I'll keep your secrets safe, your confidante and your shadow.

Please pledge to me, please promise, to be a faithful friend,
make me feel like family and love me till the end.

Keep me safe and warm, let me live inside with you,
include me when things change and hold me when I'm blue.

Kiss me when you leave, and say hello when you return,
know just who I am, and when I'm different, show concern.

If I have an accident or forget to go outside,
know I didn't mean it, I promise you, I tried.

Be my eyes and ears when my senses start to fade,
comfort my confusion, I'm aging, I'm afraid.

Please don't leave me at the end, with strangers I don't know,
when I'm taking my last breath, please be with me, please don't go.

I know it's hard for you, to see my final rest,
but I'll drift off peacefully, if I'm held gently to your chest.

I'll Meet You in the Meadow

Some say I was "just a pet," but that's not how you feel,
although I wasn't human, our heartache's just as real.

In fact, our bond was deeper, our friendship stronger too,
don't question if I felt your love, I promise you, I knew.

Separation broke our hearts, whatever was the cause,
I won't forget the last time that you held my little paws.

The last time that we snuggled, the last time that we played,
I miss the way you cared for me, I wish I could have stayed.

What we had was special, who cares how they perceive it,
our loss is overwhelming, it's okay for us to grieve it.

Our home now feels so empty, my absence is to blame,
at times you feel my presence, but I know it's not the same.

I miss you just as much you know, you meant the same to me,
but I know a place of peace, one day we will get to see.

A bridge of pretty rainbows, where animals run free,
I'll meet you in the meadow, and forever we will be.

CHAPTER THREE

THE GOOD STUFF

Quintessence of Love

Love is enduring, from summer through spring,
an endless and limitless, powerful thing.

It doesn't give up when times aren't ideal,
it's kind and it's blind and it's raw and it's real.

Love is compassion, love listens and learns,
it's gentle and tender, it's fair and takes turns.

For better or worse, when rich and when poor,
high times and low, it won't run for the door.

No judgement or ranking, accepts every flaw,
adores, reassures, makes you safe and secure.

Comforts your losses and cheers for your gains,
eases your worries, your strains and your pains.

Respects and protects, considers and cares,
thoughtful and helpful, it gives and it shares.

Love gets to know you and nurtures your soul.
Love understands and supports every goal.

Promotes peace of mind, and fills up your cup,
notices down days and picks you back up.

Intention and effort to weather each storm,
honest and true and authentic and warm.

Informs you, involves you in all of its growth,
includes and combines the worlds of you both.

Love's light will shine through, and it never gets old,
the greatest, the grandest of gifts to behold.

Dream a Dream

You're never too old to dream a new dream,
to set a new goal or to start a new scheme.

Take a small step, it's the best place to start,
the only direction, to follow your heart.

A daunting endeavour, so you must believe,
that you can achieve and that you will receive.

Step out of the zone that you're comfortable in,
reach for the sky, be in it to win.

Reach for the stars and reach for the moon,
put in the work, you'll accomplish it soon.

Enjoying the journey, a crucial component,
let yesterday's you be your only opponent.

Turn all your focus away from your fear,
have faith in yourself, you've got this my dear.

If you fumble or falter, get back on your feet,
second attempt, rinse and repeat.

Get back on the horse, stay at the controls,
action transforming your dreams into goals.

Plan it and do it, no matter what,
with all of your will and with all that you've got.

Eyes on the prize, no room to be shy,
be brave and engaged and hold your head high.

Now show off your trophy and lift up that cup,
then give thanks to you, for not giving up.

In favour of Friendship

Call on the phone or come to my door,
tell me your secrets, I'll keep them secure.

We'll laugh when we shouldn't, we'll cheer when we should,
we'll offer support through the bad times and good.

You'll forgive all my flaws, forget when I fumble,
I'll lend you a hand, pick you up when you stumble.

You'll give me advice, I won't always take heed,
but I'll always be rooting for you to succeed.

I'll listen to your troubles, you'll talk me through mine,
we'll fall out and make up, but we won't cross the line.

You'll always keep it true, even when it's hard to hear,
I'll always have your back. When you need me, I'll be near.

I'll know you inside out and you'll know me outside in,
behind your smile I'll see when your spark is wearing thin.

The trials and tribulations, the traumas and the tears,
we rode the waves together, side by side throughout the years.

I'm thankful every day for the moment we aligned,
and every moment since, bonds like this are hard to find.

That glimmer of light through a dark stormy cloud,
I call you my friend, and for that, I am proud.

You Do You

The hustle and bustle of modern-day living,
fatiguing and fierce and far from forgiving.

No respite, relief, and no time to refrain,
family, career, busy lives to sustain.

But if you refuse a breather or break,
disease will deliver a much higher stake.

Neglecting yourself, in return for your wealth,
will impact your looks, your mood and your health.

So, get lost in a book or take a long walk,
pick up the phone for a much-needed talk.

Meditate, do yoga, be mindful, clear your space,
walk barefoot in the soil, bask in the Earth's embrace.

Walk with your dogs, hang out with your cat,
fresh air and sunshine are right where it's at.

Set up some boundaries, learn to say no,
stay put, it's okay if you don't want to go.

Ask for some help, put your needs first,
eat leafy green veg, hydrate, quench your thirst.

Draw a hot bath, watch TV in bed,
log out of your socials, be present instead.

Spend time alone, with family or friends,
with no second thought about who it offends.

Rest and replenish, make time to pursue,
a moment for only what you want to do.

We simply can't pour from a bare empty cup,
with self-care and love, we must fill it up.

My Kind of Kind

Every encounter, each moment you find,
take it and make it your chance to be kind.

No need for grand gestures, no need to be bold,
a simple good deed, it's weight worth in gold.

Hold the door open, offer your seat,
smile at a stranger you meet on the street.

Compliment colleagues, ask how they are,
help stranded drivers to jump start their car.

Let someone out, let someone in,
believe in a friend, and cheer for their win.

Check on a neighbour who's old and alone,
pop in to say hi or call on the phone.

Not just for people, but all creatures too,
sparing the spider's the right thing to do.

No expectations, nothing in return,
no hidden agenda, just care and concern.

Make no announcement, put the camera away,
spread sunshine and hope and improve someone's day.

No act of kindness is ever too small,
never too late for good will to befall.

A warm-hearted gesture, a powerful tool,
the message is simple, be kind and not cruel.

You don't know what struggles or hardships they face,
or what impact we have, so be kind… Just in case.

Parenthood Misunderstood

Parenting kids, how hard can it be?
You cannot prepare; I think we'll agree.

Look in the box, there are no instructions,
who put me in charge of these little destructions?

I'll learn on the job, I'm sure I'll be fine,
I have good support from my coffee and wine.

When small hands are clenched around your big finger,
a memorable moment of magic will linger.

But not for too long, there's plenty to do,
like cleaning their vomit, their snot and their poo.

When? I don't know, for they're always awake,
hungry and crying, they don't take a break.

I'm sure when they're toddlers, it won't be as hard,
well, there is a notion to quickly discard.

Defacing my walls, walking and falling,
breaking my stuff between climbing and crawling.

Why is my kitchen now covered in lotion?
Silence more deadly than crashing commotion.

Leaving the house on time is an ask,
morning routine, an impossible task.

Tantrums in public, displeasure, knee deep,
what sane human being wants to fight off their sleep?

Surely not me, for I'm bent, broke and beat,
I can't comprehend, nor keep up or compete.

At bedtime, they're thirsty, I do feel suspicious,
weren't starving before, I'm sure it's fictitious.

But when they're unconscious, I think they're a pleasure,
so peaceful and calm, and such valuable treasure.

Reflecting on milestones, I'm thankful we share,
first words, and first steps and first cut of their hair.

It's kind of rewarding, fulfilling I feel,
I never get bored, and the love is unreal.

They're starting to stir, I crouch and crawl out,
please don't wake up, it's my only time out.

Growing up fast? Or their clothes getting smaller?
They cost me a bomb, wish they'd stop getting taller.

All they do is eat and ask for answers I don't know,
like why the sky is blue and when we die, where do we
go?

Fake laughs at their jokes, when they're not all that funny,
they do not shut up and they spend all my money.

Shopping is a chore, full of foolishness and folly,
nonsensical crap finds its way to my trolley.

Dropping them here and dropping them there,
playdates and parties, most days, everywhere.

Don't slag off the neighbour in front of your kid,
they'll rat you right out, and they'll prove that you did.

Yet another drawing of me not at my best,
still made it to the fridge, for I'm proud and truly blessed.

They also give me love notes that make my heart just burst,
their innocence is pure, they're real and unrehearsed.

They celebrate the small things, their thoughts are free and wild,
they teach me to be patient and release my inner child.

But tolerance is sparse as the teenage years creep in,
that lazy, scruffy bugger, once again, is sleeping in.

No plates left in the kitchen, they reside now in their room,
alongside seven cups, umpteen bowls, two forks, a spoon.

They hiss and grunt at me, it's like talking to the wall,
there's nothing you can tell them; they already know it all.

Missing my nice child, and counting down the days,
to when we wave goodbye to this delightful phase.

At last, it is upon us, our relationship restored,
conversation has returned, I no longer feel ignored.

We're really getting on, gotten close and made amends,
we've built a brand-new bond, not just family, now we're friends.

Parenting is hard, but it really is worthwhile,
it's not one size fits all, not one colour, not one style.

Sometimes it is terrific, sometimes it's just too tough,
we can only do our best, and hope that that's enough.

Whirlwinds of wonder we made, and we raised,
still in one piece, and for that, I'm amazed.

Elephant in the Room

The words have not been spoken, but the truth is in your eyes,
they tell me that you feel it too, yet still I analyse.

The tension, the suspension, whenever you are near,
the energy's electric and the chemistry is clear.

The catching of a look, the contact of an eye,
cloaks a common captivation, of which we may deny.

The signs, they may be subtle, but the feelings are on fire,
the language of our bodies are denoting deep desire.

An accidental touch and down my spine, there goes a shiver,
heart is skipping beats, and my legs are all a-quiver.

Each crossing of our paths, the affinity is strong,
sensing it's requited, convinced that I'm not wrong.

Silently inciteful, on the surface, still unsure,
in reality, just friends, in our dreams, a little more?

Musical Musings

Harmonious, symphonious, poetic production,
the magic of music, needs no introduction.

A comforting tonic, whatever your news,
excited, delighted, or beating the blues.

Jovial, jaunty, sharp steps or flat,
major or minor, wherever you're at.

Quiet, composed, or in need to brood,
a rhythm and range to suit every mood.

Sorrowful, sombre, or stricken with grief,
relatable lyrics to offer relief.

Brings people together and bridges the gaps,
a fleeting escape from the brink of collapse.

Reminiscent reminders can seep from a song,
endorphins released when we sing along.

A powerful piece can strike a chord,
pull at your strings or leave you floored.

Lessen your stress or move you to tears,
soothing the soul and pleasing the ears.

Shifting the tone with one single note,
a fusion of feelings, the urge to emote.

Creating a classic, a catchy arrangement,
play or perform to provide entertainment.

Donning your headphones down at the gym,
wired and inspired to feel good from within.

Raising the roof with friends at the bar,
or belting out tunes all alone in the car.

Wherever you're up to, whatever your speed,
a melody might be the measure you need.

Universally spoken, exclusively though,
so the meaning of music, only you know.

A language that's global for all to turn to,
but also assembled, uniquely for you.

CHAPTER FOUR

LADIES

One on the Way

"You're glowing" I'm told, at least ten times a day,
I'm not quite so sure, I'm not feeling that way.

I'm briming with gas, I burp and I fart,
my ankles are swollen, fatigue off the chart.

My hair has thinned out, but just on my head,
it's sprouting from everywhere else instead.

Piles are apparent, heartburn's a peach,
and I'm pretty damn sure that my poos are all breech.

Except when they're not, and fly out like a train,
either, which way, I am pressed to maintain.

Sickness is not just reserved for the morning,
at any old time, with no signal of warning.

Mithering skin, itchy and dry,
emotional wreck and I just want to cry.

My breasts are sore, and not short of a vein,
my mouth is dry, and my back is in pain.

Ironic, how many things I can't eat,
though I'm hungry enough to eat my own feet.

Don't worry, I couldn't reach if I tried,
my knees and my bump would clearly collide.

One minute, I'm craving an interesting blend,
I smell it, then nausea and vomit impend.

Sweating and cramps and I cannot sit down,
if I pee anymore, we'll all surely drown.

My legs are restless, I can't get to sleep,
cognitive slump, I can't even count sheep.

But also, I'm rammed to the rafters with pride,
for the miracle of life is growing inside.

The sound of a heartbeat, a kick in my tummy,
a gentle reminder, I'll soon be a mummy.

With every new symptom my body's expressing,
with each, an inch closer to meeting my blessing.

The Change

Ladies, let's talk about menopause,
the change of your life and the change in your drawers.

Don't suffer in silence, it's not so taboo,
it's not just a phase that you need to push through.

Let's take out the stigma, let's make them aware,
let's educate women so they can prepare,

for what Mother Nature is holding in store,
your body and mind not the same as before.

Hot flushes and headaches and itchy dry skin,
muscles and joints are now fit for the bin.

Can't get to sleep, night sweats and bad dreams,
exhausted, annoyed, and brain fog to extremes.

No thank you to sex, it hurts down below,
nunny is dry and libido is low.

Irregular cycles, till one day, no more,
anxiety high, self-esteem through the floor.

Decisions to make about HRT,
is it what's best? And is it risk free?

UTI's, they are frequent, habitual guests,
south heading and sore, your once perky breasts.

Dizzy and bloated, hair's wearing thin,
except from your ears, your nose and your chin.

Putting on weight that is harder to shift,
just who do we thank for this unwanted gift!?

Please don't be ashamed, please ask for support,
know you're still gorgeous, don't think you fall short.

Your worth has not changed, do not compare,
as much of a woman as you always were.

CHAPTER FIVE

BURDENSOME

Cash-tastrophe

Upon us, a crisis, the financial kind,
the prices are rising, our wealth has declined.

Banks raising interest to lower inflation,
a looming recession, a struggling nation.

Working to live, a thing of the past,
we work to survive; our outgoings are vast.

The mortgage has doubled, and so must the rent,
we pay what we've lent and then mostly we're spent.

Energy prices have taken a beating,
some have to choose between eating or heating.

Dinners at school, the kids will get fed,
but not when they're off, not a scrap, not a shred.

Sitting in darkness in bed to keep warm,
yesterday's nightmare, today is the norm.

No means to escape, advance, thrive or grow,
suicide high, mental health, all time low.

When childcare costs more than people are earning,
how they can work and provide is concerning.

Giving up pets, heartbroken indeed,
a part of their family, they simply can't feed.

Price caps and vouchers and schemes for support,
food banks and warm hubs are welcome resorts.

Others have more than they ever could spend,
how is it fair? I can't comprehend.

The breadline is booming, though no place to be,
action is needed, I'm sure you'll agree.

Bleak and Blue - Depression

You tell me to talk, but then when I try,
it brings down your mood, so you turn a blind eye.

My company's bleak, I'm not too much fun,
when I try to reach out, I feel like they run.

My existence is dark, I'm empty and numb,
grey clouds and black holes, down deep in my slum.

Frustration and anger stop by frequently.
Why am I here? I don't want to be.

I'm tearful and restless and riddled with guilt,
there is no escape, just the way that I'm built.

I don't see a future, just hopeless despair,
I don't want to wash for I no longer care.

I can't get to sleep, or I sleep all day long,
unworthy, inept and like I don't belong.

Feeble and fragile, in my sorry state,
just want to lie down an submit to my fate.

Thinking too much and not thinking at all,
outside I feel pain and inside I feel small.

Eating too much and not eating a bite,
cannot decide, don't know what is right.

No pleasure in life and no self-esteem,
maybe I'll wake from this sorrowful dream.

I don't want to see you, you cannot relate,
you won't understand why I cannot think straight.

You'll tell me to cheer up, and say that others have it
worse,
your positive chat just belittles my curse.

I know to drink water, I know I should talk,
to spend time in nature, to breathe and to walk.

I know to be healthy, get up and get dressed,
I know there is hope and I know that I'm blessed.

But knowing alone is not quite enough,
I can't just snap out of feeling so rough.

I'll welcome advice, but all I want here,
a kind-hearted friend with a listening ear.

Treatment and meds, they are my resort,
but from you, all I need, is just your support.

Addicted to Me

Let me introduce myself and tell you of my goal,
my name, it is addiction and I'd like to steal your soul.

I plan to take your pretty face, your dignity, your health,
I'll break down your relationships, and strip you of your wealth.

I'll rid you of your morals and I'll throw you on the shelf,
and I'll leave you just a shadow of what is your former self.

The ones you love the most, you'll leave them high and dry,
you'll steal away their peace of mind and keep them asking why.

Although, you need not worry, that's not your cross to bear,
the thirst for your dependence will outweigh how much you care.

Your pride will turn to ashes, your dreams will turn to dust,
they'll look upon you differently, pity, shame, mistrust.

I'll tell you how I operate and how I'll lure you in,
I'll approach when you are weak and when your will is wearing thin.

I'll offer an escape with a short euphoric soar,
overtake you, then forsake you and I'll leave you craving more.

Far before you fathom, you'll be trapped within my spell,
and though you'll long to leave, you'll keep on heading straight to hell.

So, avoid me at all costs and pray we never meet,
for once I sink my teeth in, I'm not easy to defeat.

But if you're truly eager to depart that downward slope,
if you only ask for help, you'll find there's always hope.

Once Upon a Narcissist

I'll make you feel so special, and I'll love bomb from the start,
we'll talk about our future, and we'll never be apart.

But please don't get too settled, this is just a phase you see,
when the honeymoon is over, how different I will be.

The pedestal you perched on, will perish pretty fast,
self-value and self-care, now mere memories from the past.

I'll start to play some games, though they won't be fun for you,
when you fell in love with me, you bit off more than you could chew.

So open and so honest, with your heart upon your sleeve,
and now I'm armed with all I need to hurt, control, deceive.

My self-esteem is low, so you see, I must persist,
to keep you in your place, your self-esteem cannot exist.

I'll make critical remarks and I'll point out all your flaws,
I'll strive to make you jealous, my need for power is the cause.

Manipulation is my forte, gaslighting is my gift,
confusion and illusion, sense of self will start to drift.

If you question me, I'll twist it, the truth you shall not claim,
you'll know not what is real, and you'll think that you're to blame.

I'll threaten to leave when I don't get my wishes,
but also effective, no contact or kisses.

Bare-bones and breadcrumbs, you'll feel the hot and cold,
I'll bait you till you bite, then I'll claim victim to your scold.

I need to be admired, and you'll find I'm always right,
arrogance, entitlement, sneaky, selfish, spite.

I have little or no empathy, I love to watch you weep,
ungrateful and unfaithful, the toxic traits I keep.

You'll never hear, "I'm sorry", I'll shift the blame to you,
defensive and offensive, and I'm better than you too.

I'll leave you feeling needy and exhausted to the core,
when you've nothing left to give, I will keep demanding more.

But when I'm through with you, I'll make it clear that I don't care,
that I've broken your poor heart and left your soul in disrepair.

I'll tell this as my story, they'll believe me over you,
for I put on quite a show, as you know, you bought it too.

Discrimin-hate

What defines discrimination?
Segregation, condemnation.

Religion, class, disability, race,
preference, gender, age, disgraced.

Unequal, unfair, hate crimes and violence,
or not so direct, the subtle, the silence.

Stand out from the masses or dare not to blend,
worth will be questioned, inclusion will end.

Rights are revoked, assumptions are made,
advantage retracted and much lower paid.

Ignored, no rewards, and needs are not met,
beaten and broken and hurt and upset.

Opportunity sparse, chance slim to none,
dignity dead, and freedom is gone.

Humanity, failing, hang heads in shame,
accept we're all equal, but not all the same.

CHAPTER SIX

FESTIVE OR NOT

Mistletoe Kisses

Winter is coming, Christmas is near,
focus on family, reflect on the year.

Give thanks for abundance, for health and for gladness,
be kind, keep in mind, the ones filled with sadness.

Make tributes and toasts to those who have gone,
good will is the season, make peace and move on.

A time for good cheer, a time to be merry,
so, force down those sprouts and get drunk on that
sherry.

Drape mantels with garlands and stockings for each,
sit round and tune in as the King makes his speech.

Tree trimmed in twinkles from head to its toe,
and topped with an angel, a star or a bow.

Baubles and bunting, tinsel and toys,
a list to tell Santa of good girls and boys.

The feeling is festive, both joyful and jolly,
evergreen wreaths dressed in ivy and holly.

The rooftops are white, and the colours are bold,
the world is lit up in red, green, and gold.

Shopping and skating and sledding together,
mittens and muffs to stay warm in cold weather.

Lie down and make angels with frosty cool snow,
stay in and sit snug around fires aglow.

Chestnuts to roast, marshmallows to toast,
greetings and meetings a-plenty to host.

Mistletoe kisses, dress up and have fun,
Elf's off the shelf, for his work here is done.

Leave pies out for Santa, and carrots for Prancer,
while kids listen closely for Rudolph and Dancer.

The magic of morning, when gifts are exchanged,
games, they are played and the table's arranged.

Dinner is served, a feast fit for a king,
crackers for pulling and carols to sing.

Time to unwind, with bellies a-brimming,
candlelight fades and the shimmer is dimming.

As we drift off to dream, just one final thought,
the meaning of Christmas is not what we bought.

Santaflaws

The trouble with Christmas, we fail to remember,
the ones drenched in dread for the month of December.

Quite conflicting feelings are potent in the air,
jolly, jaunty, joyfulness, darkness and despair.

Not all trees are tinselled, some stand bleak and bare,
no heating, no hot water, not a penny there to spare.

Santa doesn't visit poor little girls and boys,
he doesn't leave warm clothing and they don't see treats or toys.

Shopping at the foodbank, with guilt and hope and shame,
longs to feed the family but there's not much there to claim.

Some have even less, not a roof over their head,
no shelter from the wind, and nowhere safe to rest their head.

Relying on kind strangers, borrow, beg or steal,
the efforts they must go to, to obtain a basic meal.

Some are safe and warm, on their armchair, in their home,
but they're cut off from the world, with not a loved one of their own.

Loneliness, consuming, while the world outside connects,
inside, merely memories of the company they kept.

For some, it is their last, their final season here,
the festive fun is forced, but the sorrow is sincere.

Held on for what's left, and making the best,
farewells of fondness and laying to rest.

Some, deep in grief, as they have parted ways,
their loved ones were lost within months, weeks or days.

A stronger sense of longing for the ones who had to leave,
the ones they left behind with just their absence to grieve.

A time to share with loved ones, forgive and make amends,
a time to spend in company of relatives and friends.

But more time together, contrasting for each,
victims of violence, relief out of reach.

At home with their bully, no respite in sight,
no love and no light and no way to take flight.

If you cannot relate, still show that you care.
If you cannot be there, then at least spare a prayer,

for the ones who won't see anyone, for the ones outside and cold,
for the ones who won't experience the blessings that we hold.

Be thankful and be grateful, for loved ones and for wealth,
and raise a glass, not for gifts… for happiness and health.

CHAPTER SEVEN

MATTERS OF NATURE

Mother's Earth

Welcome to our earthly home, where everything's entwined,
a majestic, mighty masterpiece, both ruthless and refined.

The flora and the fauna, the nights that turn to days,
moon turning the tides, life and light from sunny rays.

From droughts to floods and downpours, where the ocean meets the land,
the wind and waves, canyons, caves, the rocks, the soil, the sand.

Survival of the fittest, the famine or the feast,
your place within the food chain, to hunt or run from beast.

Minerals in the water, and oxygen in trees,
insects cleaning up the waste, and pollinating bees.

Sun rising in the east and setting in the west,
the wonder of the weather as the seasons, they progress.

Monumental mountains, and valleys way down low,
a theatre in the sky when northern lights put on a show.

Bright colours of the rainbow, and dusky dull displays,
a misty dew, a deeper hue and hazy lazy days.

The contrast of the elements, the fire and the ice,
a rough and rugged region and a peaceful paradise.

Eruption of volcanos, the glaciers great and grand,
jungles dense and dreamy, and deserted barren land.

The thunder and the lightning, the hot springs and the
cold,
abundant and profound, a place of beauty to behold.

This world is our creator, with it we are connected,
provides for all our needs and so deserves to be
respected.

Winterful

Morning appears long before light,
hours of day, consumed by the night.

A silvery moon in a crisp clear sky,
deeply divine and the stars are not shy.

It's hard to get up, too bleak and too bitter,
too dark still for even a tweet or a twitter.

Even when dawn lends its light to the day,
the symphony softer, for most are at bay.

Some sleeping straight through this seasonal phase,
others, gone south for those warm sunny rays.

Brutal and barren for those that don't fold,
just fat, fur or feathers to fend off the cold.

Too freezing to forage, no fodder or feed,
with only their stores to survive, to succeed.

People wrapped up in soft snug attire,
hot drinks and cosy nights in by the fire.

While frigid and frosty and frozen out there,
bitter and biting, the grey gloomy air.

Windy and wet, hail rain and sleet,
thaw out your fingers and frostbitten feet.

A showboating sun, lies lucent and low,
a beautiful nightmare, a blanket of snow.

Misty and milky, flurries of ice,
a wintery wonder with views to entice.

A magical must, to keep the crust cool,
a breather for balance, to rest and refuel.

To restore and renew, we forsake and forgo,
consequentially crucial, our friend, not our foe.

Spring in my step

A warmer wave, a thawing chill,
sprouting, springs first daffodil.

Life returns, renewed, reborn,
euphonical debut, thrush at dawn.

Buzzing bees, balmy breeze,
fragrant, fresh, frondescent trees.

Blankets of bluebells, meadows of green,
charming and calming, seductive, serene.

Sunshine and rainbows and thunderstorm showers,
explosions of colour that burst into flowers.

Blossoms of cherry, tulips and heather,
bountiful bliss from a fusion of weather.

New baby lambs and bunnies arrive,
ambience ample for wee ones to thrive.

Fresh hope and fresh chances, new starts and new
dreams.
the wonder of life and what spring truly means.

Summershsine

Four in the morning, twilight is here,
dawn is approaching, sunrise is near.

When all's calm and quiet, when no one's around,
wildlife awakens, birds softly sound.

The long day that follows the first sign of light,
seeps in and succeeds the short summer night.

The sun nestles high in the blue cloudless sky,
copious crops in abundant supply.

Fruitful and fertile, flourishing fauna,
life is emerging from corner to corner.

Bask on the beach, play in the park,
frolicking alfresco while the light outshines the dark.

Grilling in the garden, lounging in the shade,
ice pops, flip flops, beer and lemonade.

BBQs and sun cream, and grass that's freshly mowed,
fragrant and familiar, seasons scents boldly bestowed.

Ravishing, the rainbows, that sweep across your view,
vibrantly and vividly reflecting from the dew.

Sultry and sweet, lavish and lush,
evening draws in, the air calm and hush.

A sapphire sky, now dusky and deep,
the sun in all her splendour as she slumbers into sleep.

Falling for autumn

As the hot summer cycle bids us farewell,
an enchanted earth casts an Autumnal spell.

A symbolic shift, a reminder to rest,
the temperature drops but the trees are undressed.

A low golden sun, a bright harvest moon,
blustery mornings and wet afternoons.

Misty warm breath against crisp chilly air.
Winter's enroute, it's time to prepare.

Migrating birds are flocking for flight,
dens are compiled for the long sleepy night.

Berries and nuts, they stock and they store,
if they want to survive, they must take on this chore.

Harvesting humans pick apples for pies,
collect all the crops before everything dies.

Crackling fires and sweet sticky s'mores,
brollys and boots and coats for outdoors.

Patches of pumpkins, witches and ghosts,
hot chocolate and cider for seasonal toasts.

A magical glance at a dazzling display,
branches laid bare as the trees dance and sway.

Crunchy bronze leaves enshrouding the ground,
a palette of plenty, pronounced and profound.

Amongst the earthy tones and shades,
rich notes of amber and blush cascades.

Sandalwood and cinnamon, with hints of rain and spice,
musky, mild and mellow, aromatic paradise.

A season of profusion, that really hits the spot.
Falling for Autumn? How could you not.

A Climate in Crisis

The climate is in crisis, the earth is in a bind,
our planet's in a pickle at the hands of humankind.

Burning fossil fuels like oil and gas and coal,
the reason for the ozone's ultraviolet seeping hole.

Greenhouse gas emissions, generated on repeat,
form a wrap around our world and trap in all the heat.

Warmth wanders to the waters, forcing oceans to expand,
the rising of the sea, contradicts the coast's command.

Ice sheets reflect energy from the sun back into space,
when they've melted into memories, we'll endure her true
embrace.

Eternal microplastics polluting the deep blue,
altering the chemistry, result? A deadly brew.

Many living beings mistake plastic for a meal,
suffocation and entanglement, it's happening, it's real.

Industry and transport on the rise from high demand,
deforestation of our trees, for cows and crops, and land.

Ending eco systems, emitting C02,
wildlife losing loved ones, their homes and all they knew.

The temperature is rising, we feel it in the air,
some basking in the sun, for some, a dangerous affair.

Heatwaves drawing droughts, or a host to rampant rain,
floods from bursting banks or from an overpowered drain.

Catastrophic storms leave the region bent and broke,
corrosion of the shorelines, relocation of its folk.

Landslides and tsunamis and the spread of fatal fire,
are presents from the present, but the future's much more dire.

Deserts will expand, no means for food and drink,
too sweltering to work, survival on the brink.

Climate refugees will flee those bare and barren places,
animals as well, will share these overcrowded spaces.

Some won't make it though, they'll die along the way,
extinction will increase, devastation every day.

Conditions cataclysmic and daunting to the core,
beyond imagination, like we've never seen before.

We're on our final warning, we're on our final chance,
we're the final generation that can ditch this dreary dance.

Cut down your carbon footprint, take the bike and not the car,
reduce, reuse, recycle, buy from local not afar.

Don't waste away your water, when you're clean, get out the shower,
choose eco-friendly products, light your home with solar power.

Unplug what you're not using, give standby mode the chop,
plant some trees, save the bees, take your own bag to the shop.

Eat less meat and dairy, take the stairs and not the lift,
research what you can do, for knowledge is a gift.

If each and every one of us would show some real concern,
we might be able to avoid the point of no return.

CHAPTER EIGHT

POINTS TO PONDER

Pointless Pursuit

Running around and around on a wheel,
does this seem a little like how you might feel?

A pointless pursuit in search of success,
to dress to impress and for things to possess.

But some are employed, not even to thrive,
to live day by day, to get by, to survive.

Repeating a cycle to buy basic bits,
plodding along in monotonous pits.

Wake up and get dressed and then head off to work,
blood, sweat and tears, for barely a perk.

Head home, have a shower, put on your night
gown,
an hour or two, to eat and wind down.

Head off to bed and switch off your brain,
up early tomorrow to do it again.

The daily grind will take its toll,
decay your mind and drain your soul.

Work, sleep, repeat, a gruelling rotation,
though we have been granted two days of salvation.

Two days to enjoy with your friends or your spouse,
but not before shopping and cleaning the house.

So much to do and in such a short span,
what time was spent on your personal plan?

Too busy for leisure, too jaded for pleasure,
we still must partake as it pays for our treasure.

To purchase a home that is barely lived in,
to finance a car you don't take for a spin.

Drive it to work and then drive it back home,
then slog out your guts just to pay off the loan.

We're stuck in the system, it's hard to break free,
affording our lifestyle is all we can see.

But we're all the same, so it must be okay,
that we're under control to comply and obey.

Imagine a world, where we all took a stand,
refused to partake and ignored their command.

Lived wild and free and altered the pace,
and simply bowed out of this wretched rat race.

Digital dilemma

Advancement, enhancement, the digital age,
sharing our lives with the world, all the rage.

Get social with media, put on a show,
pretend life is perfect and they'll never know.

Argue with strangers, while sitting alone,
miss out on the moment, stare at your phone.

Give details to scammers, your mothers last name,
these questions are asked and disguised as a game.

Say cheese, flip your lens, and aim it at you,
the selfie's arrived and the filters have too.

Crop them and chop them and straighten them out,
nothing on news feeds but faces with pouts.

Get enough likes on your content online,
defining your worth, a disturbing design.

ATM's and self-check outs have claimed our careers,
anxiety rising, phobias, fears.

Kids cooped in their room in a fantasy land,
strangers for friends, social skills won't expand.

Disinformation and spread of fake news,
gambling, porn, and much more to misuse.

Not all doom and gloom, some positives too,
banking and shopping from home with no queue.

Selection of channels, what shall we watch?
programmes on tap, entertainment, top notch.

Booking a break, or a coach or a show,
stuck on a question? Google will know.

Courses online to improve your credentials,
profiles for dating, weigh up the potentials.

Video calls from wherever you are,
keeping in contact with friends wide and far.

If you're happy or not with this digital day,
technology's here, it won't go away.

Embrace it, enjoy it, but do not abuse,
its value is raised, when we don't overuse.

.

Covid O' clock

On the news, a new story, a viral affair,
but what was to come, we were far from aware.

At first, not to panic, it's not our concern,
just the flu, just in China, well that took a turn.

A global emergency soon was declared,
and then came the closure of borders we shared.

Travel restricted, where once we could roam,
then out of the blue, we could barely get home.

But that came too late, and it spread far and wide,
without further ado, the pandemic arrived.

Just two weeks were needed, to make the curve flat,
two years down the line and that's not where we sat.

Looking back at our journey and what we went through,
scientists and Boris, FDA and the WHO.

Lock downs and meltdowns, staying in to save lives,
seeing the rate of the suicides rise.

Vulnerable kids stuck at home in depression,
no means of escape from domestic aggression.

Panic buying loo roll and emptying the shelf,
time slots for key workers and for elders in poor health.

Bubbles of support and households couldn't mix,
permitted to the park in groups of two, or groups of six.

Keeping social distanced, to help control the spread,
at least two metres apart to avoid the viral shed.

Some of us were furloughed, some worked from their
home,
some just made it through, some lost everything they
owned.

We ate out to help out, but little did that do,
big companies went bust and small businesses fell
through.

Hospitality and travel were brought down to their knees,
the high street never made it, lost its fight to this disease.

Kids were super spreaders, home schooling was a chore,
we clapped hands for our heroes standing tearful at
our door.

We wore face masks to save others,
our neighbours, friends, and mothers.

Hand gels, they were sold, PPE like finding gold,
"hands, face, space" the message frequently was told.

The green list or the amber, to go somewhere offshore,
PCR's and LFD's and tiers from one to four.

We queued up for our vaccines, for one, two and three,
but new variants arrived, and we went then to plan B.

Time in isolation was difficult to bear,
but what about the ones who spent the whole two years there?

Some had flu-like symptoms, some lost their taste and smell,
others on their death beds, no loved ones, no farewell.

We couldn't visit care homes, their zest for life was low,
the few staff that they had tried to give them back their glow.

Though, for some it was too much, their time to pass was clear,
in the kind arms of the carer, their poor family nowhere near.

One thing that is for certain, one thing we'll all agree,
though haunted by the memories, we're happy to be free.

Miracle of Me

Do you know about me? I'm a human here on Earth,
I came into this world before my date and time of birth.

I lived inside the womb of another living being,
her body kept me safe and warm until my time of fleeing.

My existence is a marvel, a challenge to perceive,
what networks synchronising in succession can achieve.

I am a single structure, made up of billions more,
tissues, systems, cells and my organs are the four.

Elements and energy, fat, water and blood,
countless interactions, joining forces as they should.

My head, my neck, my torso, my limbs, and hands, and feet,
are visible components, the rest, somewhat, discreet.

So look a little closer, I'm much more than what you've seen,
I'm the miracle of life, I am an intricate machine.

My skin sits on the surface of all that lies beneath,
it covers me from head to toe, my own protective sheath.

Shields from loss of moisture, infection, heat and light,
sensory receptors to protect with all their might.

Muscles help me move, they're always on the go,
driving blood around, affects the pressure and the flow.

One muscle is my hero, working harder than the rest,
my heart beats at all times and nestles safely in my chest.

It uses many vessels to pump my blood around,
where oxygen and nutrients and hormones can be found.

My nose sits on my face and provides my sense of smell,
it warms and moistens air outside and filters it as well.

It draws in only oxygen and makes its journey slick,
through my windpipe to my lungs, its occurrence, calm
and quick.

Carbon monoxide is extracted from my blood stream,
have no doubt,
rejected and removed with every breath that I let out.

My mouth has many jobs, filled with buds to taste my
food,
canines chew it up, saliva moves it through my tubes.

Straight into my stomach, breaks it down and sends it on,
into my small intestine measuring five metres long.

Absorbs the stuff that's good, and the rest is thrown
away,
how I know it's working? At least two poos a day.

My skeleton supports me, my shape, posture and frame,
safeguards internal organs, my spinal cord and brain.

Marrow making blood cells, storing minerals in my bones,
two hundred and six to be exact, split in two different
zones.

Instigating muscles, attached at certain points,
facilitate my movement at my bone connecting joints.

My bones, they are self-healing, my liver is the same,
but let's dedicate a moment to the function of my brain.

My brain and I are close, it knows me inside out,
controls at every level, what I feel or think about.

Decides when I am hungry, when I'm cold and what I
learn,
in charge of what I see, when I breath, for whom I yearn.

It locks away my memories for as and when I need,
tells me if I'm poorly, and in which way to proceed.

Regulates my functions, it tells me when to move,
manages my mood and if I do or don't approve.

Sends signals to each organ, every system, everywhere,
it is my higher power, it's my hard drive and software.

I'm taller in the morning, I'm shorter in the night,
I sense when there is danger and respond with fight or
flight.

My fingers each have prints that are unique to me,
microbes reside both in and out, germ free to no degree.

Ears give me balance, they help me hear your voice,
they'll grow until I die, as will my nose, I have no choice.

Water makes up more than half of every pound I weigh.
On average I take in and out two thousand breaths a day.

My parts that come in pairs, I can live with only one,
exclusively distinctive, no replacement when I am gone.

A format that is flawless, a life promoting land,
arrangement of connections, so complex, it must be
planned.

Now look into the mirror, and find yourself star-struck,
a prodigy, a sight to see, on purpose, not by luck.

Regret Me Not

Life's short, buy the shoes,
don't waste time on rueful blues.

Jump in puddles, take the trip,
from life's cup, just have a sip.

Don't look back, it's been and done,
except to see how far you've come.

Throw caution to the wind, I say,
treat life like it's your last day.

Don't hold back, sing and dance.
A leap of faith, a risk, a chance.

Make the most, seize the day,
don't just work, make time for play.

Chase your dreams, believe in you,
have faith in everything you do.

Drive the sports car, take the wheel,
make a difference, make the deal.

If you love them, tell them so,
unless you say it, they won't know.

Learn your lessons, set you free,
let go of thinking what could be.

Drop the grudge, forgive, forget,
don't leave this earth with one regret.

Right on Time

Is time an illusion? Is time a dimension?
It's up when it's up, no granted extension.

Just our perception? Or actually so?
That it flies when you're high and stands still when you're low.

Tick tock on the clock, moving forward in motion,
exclusively onward, unbroken devotion.

Switch off the alarm and silence the chime,
you can turn back the hands, but you can't turn back time.

It won't wait or delay, stand still or take pause,
whoever you are or whatever your cause.

Not to be seen, you can't touch, smell or taste it,
and though it's not yours, you can spend, keep or waste it.

It cannot be found, once lost, gone forever,
a timeless pursuit and an endless endeavour.

CHAPTER NINE

A LIGHTER BITE

Cast of the Conference Call

Assigned to the conference, enrolled on the course,
charge your device, let's meet the workforce.

Type in your PIN, it's time to log in,
your meeting online is about to begin.

Sit down at your tablet, your phone or computer,
join in the call and let's meet your tutor.

A grid full of guests, a mad pantomime,
the same old dynamics, each single time.

Top left, there is Sue, who knows not what to do,
technology's new and she's not got a clue.

Logs in then logs out, screen's clear then distorted,
she'll hold up the show till she finally gets sorted.

Bob's bottom right and his signal is shite,
he'll try to stay with us with all of his might.

From start to the end, both lost and connected,
distraction to which we will all be subjected.

Sheila is shy, no picture or sound,
does she exist? Nowhere to be found.

Janet has jobs that simply can't wait,
we'll all sit and watch while she empties her plate.

Dishes and ironing, nothing forbidden,
plucking her chin hair, zero is hidden.

The entrance of Ted, says he's fresh out of bed,
clean hair for Carol, a towel on her head.

Michael, the mime, his mic's off again,
his mouth is in motion, he's trying to explain.

He's been told ten times, that we can't hear a word,
most of his input is seen but not heard.

The forehead of Frank is all that we'll meet,
just background for Bee, has she fell off her seat?

Dressed to impress, Deb's dolled up to death,
nightwear and slippers, for Jeff, Beth and Seth.

Cathy drinks coffee, John has the jokes,
Wendy drinks wine, while Fred freely smokes.

Stan is a statue, he may not be real,
we'll watch Dave devour a full three course meal.

Harry's home is hectic, no chaos can compare,
TV loud, a busy crowd, wreaking havoc there.

Deliveries a-plenty, kids and pets galore,
discord and disorder like you've never seen before.

Then there is the one we secretly detest,
chitter chatter Charley, more rampant than the rest.

He's keen with all the answers, and fond of his own
voice,
many questions at the end, we'll wait, we have no choice.

Impatient sighs, we want goodbyes,
instead, a group of rolling eyes.

Then one by one, the gang is gone,
thank you all for logging on.

Holibobs

I had an idea, let's go on our jollies,
it will be simple, no faux pas or follies.

We'll book it online, it will be fine,
we'll wade through the web for a budget airline.

A bargain we've found, these flights are so cheap,
but upwards and fast, the charges they creep.

Taking a case, it comes at a cost,
then to insure it in case it gets lost.

To sit with companions, you'll have to pay,
if they can fleece you, they'll find a way.

Charges for toilets, you may not believe,
I wouldn't be shocked if they charged us to breathe.

Booking confirmed, the kids will be thrilled,
why wouldn't they be? They're not getting billed!

They'll mither for months, till we're out the door,
packing, repacking, then questions, then more.

The time is approaching for us to prepare,
so much to do before heading off there.

A list to check off, but where to begin?
The house must be gleaming while no one is in.

What's to be packed is not quite agreed,
someone will forget at least one thing we need.

Clothes for the morning and clothes for the night,
clothes "just in case" and then clothes for the flight.

Bring sweets and games, they're good for the plane,
I'm sure all that sugar won't send them insane.

In each group there is the responsible one,
does all the work while the others look on.

Passports and tickets, secure in their care,
the rest getting by on a wing and a prayer.

The day has arrived, hip hip hooray,
a frantic, erratic, chaotic display.

One final check in complete disarray,
the taxi was late but now we're on our way.

The traffic is gridlocked, we're stuck in a jam,
these kids keep on fighting, I'm soon to go ham.

Thank goodness, we're here, let's go and check in,
we didn't online, so a fee for our sin.

Luggage too heavy, too big for the scales,
you guessed it, a payment, is what that entails.

Security far from an orderly manner,
shoes and belts off and then walk through the scanner.

It beeps, you're instructed to take off some more,
back through, then a frisking and search to endure.

We did it, we made it, now straight to the pub,
a pint, pretty standard, and overpriced grub.

Packed full of people for far-away places,
shops selling sandals and caftans and cases.

Called to the gate and welcomed on board,
faffing and nesting and hand luggage stored.

Kicking the seat of the tough nut in front,
"Stop that right now," before I take the brunt.

Bickering adults and vomit in bags,
crew up the wall with a group of drunk stags.

We've got here, we made it, excitement kicks in,
we're here on our jollies, now where to begin.

Find our resort, our home for the week,
get settled in, explore and critique.

Hang up our garments, live out of the trunk,
head to the pool bar, try not to get drunk.

Sunscreen the children, lay it on thick,
time in the shade, so no one gets sick.

Sunshine is hot and the aircon is cool,
blow up the lilo and jump in the pool.

All is inclusive, with soft drinks on tap,
the cocktails excluded are watered down crap.

The buffet, top drawer, we cannot complain,
diet, diminished, no chance I'll refrain.

Lilo's deflated, that didn't last long,
ice creams are melting, well what could go wrong?

A club just for kids, so we get a break,
our brief bit of peace, for the children's own sake.

A day at the beach is part of the plan,
castles of sand while we work on our tan.

A gentle sea breeze as waves hit the shore,
the sky, clear and blue and a view to adore.

I pulled out three books I had planned to read,
a pipe dream that died when I chose to breed.

At our hotel, entertainment gets going,
cabaret showing and wine freely flowing.

As our last night draws to its end,
our time to check out, is soon to impend.

Reflecting on moments that we've spent together,
pictures and memories that we'll hold forever.

The children, the luggage and even my spouse,
safely back home to our spotless clean house.

Ten loads of washing piled up to there,
post-holiday blues that I simply can't bear.

And though once or twice, I sure did complain,
let's book another and do it again.

The Middle of Age

Here we are, the middle of being,
now when we're laughing, we're probably peeing.

Coughing or sneezing, the same situation,
zero control of our own urination.

Too old for clubbing, too young to play bowls,
a panicky push to accomplish our goals.

As still as can be, we'll put out our back,
our knees are now noisy, they crunch, creak and crack.

It's hard to get up and it's hard to get down,
crows' feet when we smile, and folds when we frown.

Wrinkles and crinkles and jowls at the jaw,
shifting that timber, much more of a chore.

The handrail, a feature we've started to use,
we now qualify to consider a cruise.

Style after comfort and board games are fun,
Madam and Sir, we now have become.

As soon as we sit, a nap will commence,
you may still be talking, please don't take offence.

Glasses for reading and glasses for wine,
not clever online and we're in bed by nine.

Cannot remember what we came to do,
not cool like we were, the lingo's all new.

But wisdom's our thing, we're worldly and wise,
we are who we are, no pretence or disguise.

We live for the moment; we know life's a gift,
priorities making a meaningful shift.

A spoken truth, with value unsung,
youth really is wasted, when spent on the young.

Oh to be British

Good evening old chap, what can I say?
Lend us an ear, for it's been quite a day.

The church bells, they woke me, along with the lark,
the cold, cobbled streets, still deserted and dark.

I arose from my bed at that silly hour,
kettle went on and I hopped in the shower.

I looked out the window, the weather was grey,
hat, coat and boots, I was dressed for the day.

The café I called to, second to none,
my order, routine, a full English for one.

But today, in the queue, a man jumped right in,
I was livid and cross, and my patience were thin.

I told him, "I'm sorry", though it wasn't my blunder,
"Please go to the back", well he stormed off like thunder.

With a stiff upper lip, and polite as can be,
next time he'll know not to trifle with me.

After my brekkie, I walked out the door,
the weather had changed and was not like before.

The sun, it was shining, the temperature rose,
I quickly nipped home and changed out of those clothes.

T-shirt and shorts as the weather was fine,
I took my chance, hung a wash on the line.

Then I bobbed to the beach, the shoreline was rammed,
sun cream on faces and screwballs in hand.

Within less than an hour, the weather turned sour,
the rain, it danced down and was more than a shower.

I legged it back home, rushed my washing inside,
sat by the fire, drank tea and got dried.

Back in my coat with my brolly close by,
I popped to the pub for a pint and a pie.

I held the door open for a lady and gent,
with no thanks from either, straight through it they went.

"You're welcome!" I muttered, in sarcastic tone,
shook my head and moved on, as I don't like to moan.

Countryside views and a jolly old host,
fresh out of pie so I went for the roast.

Then, biscuity bourbons and tea by the pot,
I extended my pinky and drank the whole lot.

I went to the market to walk off my meal,
browsed through the stalls and I bartered a steal.

I ran into some fellows and stopped for a natter,
sports and the weather, the usual chatter.

On my way home after doing the rounds,
I fetched a fish supper for twelve English pounds.

I brought it back home to fill up my belly,
I sat on the couch, watching soaps on the telly.

Slippers and pipe, with a night cap in hand,
farewell there old chap, for I'm off to dreamland.

Wide Awake Club

The hour is late and bedtime is calling,
drowsy and dozy, I'm fighting but falling.

Rest on my pillow and snuggle right in,
then, ping, something, somewhere awakens within.

My head's many voices are deep in debate,
I have vital questions; the answers can't wait.

Like, how to make cheese? Do penguins have knees?
A full list of everything that grows on trees.

Let's check online, I need to know now,
why are we here? Where? When? And how?

A list that's, "to do" for when I'm awake,
let's get to sleep first, for bloody hell's sake.

What should I do? I hope it's not raining,
in a few hours, I'll sure be complaining.

But here in this moment, in this early hour,
what would I change first, if I were in power?

Now I'm not thinking, but still wide awake,
please go to sleep brain and give me a break.

My eyes won't stay open, they're heavy, like lead,
but I'm just a sleepy, awake fool in bed.

I'm finally drifting, oh, here I go,
then, bing, a reply from three hours ago.

I will ignore it, for I'm trying to rest,
or check just in case it's an urgent request.

Let's count some sheep, I'm sure that's the key,
slip into slumber…. Now I need to pee.

This taxing rotation endures through the night,
then out for the count when approaching dawn's light.

Alarm clock engages, no, not a chance,
I guess we'll be playing the snooze button dance.

I cannot get up, ain't that the way,
now I could sleep for the rest of the day.

Insomnia, callous and far from contrite,
an unwanted guest that checks in every night.

!

THANK YOU

Printed in Great Britain
by Amazon

29897219R00069